SUCCESSFUL COOKING

WEEKNIGHT MEALS

INDEX

Contents

Weeknight Meals

After a long day at work, slaving over a hot stove is often the last thing you feel like doing. But, armed with a well-stocked kitchen and the following ideas, you'll have dinner ready in no time.

Weeknight Meals offers a selection of evening meals for four people that are quick to prepare, feature a short list of ingredients (readily available from most large supermarkets) and, most importantly, are full of flavour. To save you time, we've kept preparation time for all recipes to 15 minutes or less.

Organisation is the key to cooking a variety of convenient and tasty workday meals – a pantry well-stocked with staples is a must. 'Pantry staples' are non-perishable products common to many recipes such as flour, canned tomatoes and dried herbs, and those that make versatile accompaniments (rice, pasta and couscous). Restock your pantry when these items are getting low (see suggestions on facing page).

Maintaining a good supply of dry and canned ingredients, oils, herbs and spices is a great start, but let's not forget to replenish the refrigerator with fresh produce – vegetables, dairy products, meat, poultry and seafood. Fresh ingredients are essential in making up a balanced meal.

Now that the pantry is full and there is a constant supply of fresh ingredients, the weekday cook has the flexibility to plan in advance for the week's meals or to decide on the spur of the moment what's on tonight's dinner menu.

STORE CUPBOARD INGREDIENTS

- beans, canned
- breadcrumbs, dry
- capers
- coconut milk
- couscous
- curry pastes
- flour, plain
- flour, self-raising
- Italian tomato passata, bottled
- mustard (Dijon, wholegrain)
- noodles
- nuts
- oil – it is a good idea to have two types of oil in your pantry at all times; olive oil is good for

Mediterranean cooking and salad dressings, while a good all-purpose vegetable or seed oil such as sunflower oil is suitable for general cooking purposes and more compatible to Asian flavours than the distinct flavour of olive oil.

- oyster sauce
- pasta
- polenta
- rice
- salmon, canned
- soy sauce
- spices
- stock (in tetra packs)
- sugar, caster
- sugar, soft brown
- sweet chilli sauce
- tomato paste
- tomatoes, canned
- tuna, canned
- vinegars (balsamic, red wine, white wine, herb infused)

STORAGE

When stored well, packet ingredients should last until their use-by date. Once you have opened packages, remember to seal them properly or store the contents in well-labelled airtight containers.

Check the labels after opening jars of sauces and condiments to ensure they don't require refrigeration after opening. To store pastes (such as tomato and curry) for longer periods of time in convenient small portions, spoon into ice-cube trays, freeze, divide into plastic bags and keep in the freezer until ready to use.

TIME-SAVING TIPS

- Find a good local butcher who pre-dices and slices high-quality meat cuts. This saves not only time but also paying for fat and sinew that you will discard anyway (although take care as some pre-cut meat can be fatty and not at its peak).
- It is handy to have a ready supply of ingredients that are the flavour base for a vast range of meals, in particular garlic, onions, ginger and chillies. Whenever possible, using fresh varieties of these are best as their flavour is far superior to the bottled versions.
- Stocks are a common liquid base to many dishes and, for optimum flavour, it is often recommended to make your own. Good-quality liquid stocks, however, can be purchased and are available in tetra packs or in cans. Canned stocks are available from Asian stores or in the Asian section of most large supermarkets.
- Plan ahead: read through your recipe and get out all the equipment and ingredients that you need, before you start.
- Decide on any side dishes or accompaniments you wish to serve, and where possible, prepare them while cooking the main meal. Many dishes such as stir-fries, curries and pan-fries are accompanied by rice, which takes about 15 minutes to cook. To maximise time usage, start cooking the rice before you start preparing the rest of your meal.

Spaghettini with Asparagus and Rocket

PREPARATION TIME: 15 minutes
COOKING TIME: 15 minutes
SERVES 4

100 ml extra virgin olive oil
16 thin asparagus spears, cut into
  5 cm lengths
375 g spaghettini
120 g rocket, shredded
2 small fresh red chillies, finely chopped
2 teaspoons finely grated lemon rind
1 clove garlic, finely chopped
1 cup (100 g) grated Parmesan
2 tablespoons lemon juice

1 Bring a large saucepan of water to the boil over medium heat. Add 1 tablespoon of the oil and a pinch of salt to the water and blanch the asparagus for 3–4 minutes. Remove the asparagus with a slotted spoon, refresh under cold water, drain and place in a bowl. Return the water to a rapid boil and add the spaghettini. Cook the pasta according to the packet instructions until al dente. Drain and return to the pan.

2 Meanwhile, add the rocket, chilli, lemon rind, garlic and ⅔ cup (65 g) of the Parmesan to the asparagus and mix well. Add the mixture to the cooked pasta, pour on the lemon juice and the remaining olive oil and season with salt and freshly ground black pepper. Stir well to evenly coat the pasta with the mixture. Divide among four pasta bowls, top with the remaining Parmesan and serve.

Once blanched, refresh asparagus under cold running water.

Mix together asparagus, rocket, chilli, lemon rind and garlic.

7

Pasta with Pork and Fennel Sausages

PREPARATION TIME: 15 minutes
COOKING TIME: 40 minutes
SERVES 4

6 Italian pork and fennel sausages
  (about 550 g)
1 tablespoon olive oil
1 small red onion, finely chopped
2–3 cloves garlic, crushed
½ teaspoon chilli flakes
300 g field or button mushrooms, thinly
  sliced
2 x 400 g cans diced tomatoes
1 tablespoon finely chopped fresh thyme
500 g penne rigate
grated Parmesan, to serve

1 Split the sausages open, remove and crumble the filling, then discard the skins.

2 Heat the oil in a large saucepan over medium–high heat and cook the onion for 3–4 minutes, or until fragrant and transparent. Add the garlic, chilli flakes, mushrooms and crumbled sausage meat. Cook over high heat, stirring gently to mash the sausage meat, for 4–5 minutes, or until the meat is evenly browned. If necessary, use a tablespoon to remove any excess fat from the pan, leaving about a tablespoon of oil. Continue to cook, stirring once or twice, for 10 minutes.

3 Stir in the tomato and thyme, then bring the sauce to the boil. Cover and cook over medium–low heat for 20 minutes, stirring occasionally to make sure the sauce doesn't stick to the bottom of the pan.

4 Meanwhile, cook pasta in a large saucepan of rapidly boiling salted water according to the packet instructions until al dente. Drain well, then add to the sauce, stirring gently to combine. Garnish with Parmesan, then serve with a green salad.

Split sausages open, remove and crumble filling, and discard skins.

Cook sausage meat over high heat, stirring to crumble meat.

Chicken and Mushroom Pilau

PREPARATION TIME: 15 minutes +
30 minutes standing
COOKING TIME: 35 minutes
SERVES 4

1½ cups (300 g) basmati rice
2 tablespoons oil
1 large onion, chopped
3–4 cloves garlic, crushed
1 tablespoon finely chopped fresh ginger
500 g chicken tenderloin fillets, trimmed
  and cut into small pieces
300 g Swiss brown mushrooms, sliced
¾ cup (90 g) slivered almonds, toasted
1½–2 teaspoons garam masala, dry roasted
½ cup (125 g) plain yoghurt
1 tablespoon finely chopped fresh coriander
  leaves
fresh coriander leaves, extra, to garnish

1 Rinse the rice under cold water until the water runs clear. Drain and leave for 30 minutes. Heat the oil in a large saucepan over medium heat and stir in the onion, garlic and ginger. Cook, covered, for 5 minutes, or until the onion is browned. Increase the heat to high, add the chicken and cook, stirring, for 3–4 minutes, or until the chicken is lightly browned.

2 Stir in the mushrooms, almonds and garam masala. Cook, covered, for another 3 minutes, or until the mushrooms are soft. Remove the lid and cook, stirring, for 2 minutes, or until the liquid evaporates. Remove the chicken pieces from the pan.

3 Add the rice to the pan and stir for 30 seconds, or until well coated in the mushroom and onion mixture. Pour in 1½ cups (375 ml) water and bring to the boil, stirring frequently to prevent the ingredients catching on the bottom of the pan. Cook for 2 minutes, or until most of the water has evaporated. Return the chicken to the pan, reduce the heat to low and steam, covered, for 15 minutes, or until the rice is cooked.

4 Meanwhile, combine the yoghurt and chopped coriander in a small bowl. Fluff the rice with a fork, then divide among serving bowls. Top with a dollop of the yoghurt mixture and garnish with coriander leaves.

Add chicken to onion, garlic and ginger and cook until browned.

Linguine with Chargrilled Basil and Lemon Seafood

PREPARATION TIME: 15 minutes +
10 minutes marinating
COOKING TIME: 15 minutes
SERVES 4

16 raw medium prawns, peeled and
   deveined, with tails intact
350 g calamari rings
½ cup (125 ml) extra virgin olive oil
⅓ cup (80 ml) lemon juice
3 cloves garlic, crushed
½ teaspoon chilli flakes
3 tablespoons chopped fresh basil
400 g linguine
1 teaspoon grated lemon rind

1 Place the prawns and calamari in a non-metallic dish. To make the dressing, combine the olive oil and lemon juice in a small jug, then pour ¼ cup (60 ml) into a small bowl, reserving the rest. Stir the garlic, chilli flakes and 2 tablespoons of the basil into the bowl, pour over the seafood and mix to coat well. Cover with plastic wrap and marinate in the refrigerator for 5–10 minutes.

2 Cook the pasta in a large saucepan of rapidly boiling salted water according to the packet instructions until al dente. Drain, then return to the pan.

3 Meanwhile, preheat a chargrill pan to high and brush with oil. Remove the prawns from the marinade with tongs and cook for 2–3 minutes each side, or until pink and cooked through. Remove. Add the calamari in batches and cook, turning once, for 1–3 minutes, or until opaque and cooked through—take care not to overcrowd the chargrill pan.

4 Transfer the pasta to a large serving bowl, then add the seafood, lemon rind and reserved dressing and gently toss together until the linguine is well coated. Garnish with the remaining basil and season to taste. Serve with a rocket salad.

Orecchiette with Mushrooms, Pancetta and Smoked Mozzarella

PREPARATION TIME: 10 minutes
COOKING TIME: 15 minutes
SERVES 4

400 g orecchiette
2 tablespoons olive oil
150 g sliced pancetta, cut into short thin strips
200 g button mushrooms, sliced
2 leeks, sliced
1 cup (250 ml) cream
200 g smoked mozzarella (mozzarella affumicata), cut into 1 cm cubes
8 fresh basil leaves, roughly torn

1 Cook the pasta in a large saucepan of rapidly boiling salted water according to the packet instructions until al dente.

2 Meanwhile, heat the oil in a large frying pan and sauté the pancetta, mushrooms and leek over medium–high heat for 5 minutes. Stir in the cream and season with pepper—the pancetta should provide enough salty flavour. Simmer over low heat for 5 minutes, or until the pasta is ready. Drain the pasta and stir into the frying pan. Add the mozzarella and basil and toss lightly.

Sauté pancetta, mushrooms and leek, then stir in cream and pepper.

Fried Rice with Chinese Barbecue Pork

PREPARATION TIME: 15 minutes
COOKING TIME: 10 minutes
SERVES 4

6 spring onions
150 g snow peas
200 g Chinese barbecue pork
3 teaspoons sesame oil
2 eggs, lightly beaten
2 cloves garlic, finely chopped
3 cups (555 g) cold cooked white long-grain
   rice
2 tablespoons soy sauce

1 Cut the spring onions and snow peas diagonally into very thin shreds. Cut the pork into thin slices.

2 Heat a wok until hot, add 1 teaspoon of the oil and swirl to coat the base. Add the egg and swirl over the base until just set. Turn over and cook for 30 seconds, or until just lightly browned, then remove from the wok. Allow the egg to cool slightly, then roll up and cut into 1 cm thick slices.

3 While the wok is still very hot, add the remaining oil, then the garlic, spring onion and snow peas and stir-fry for 1–2 minutes, or until slightly soft. Add the pork, rice, soy sauce and strips of omelette and toss until heated through and thoroughly combined—the soy sauce should turn the rice brown. Remove from the heat and serve immediately.

Add egg to very hot wok, swirl to coat thinly until just set.

While wok is still very hot, add spring onions and snow peas.

Baked Prawn Risotto with Thai Flavours

PREPARATION TIME: 15 minutes
COOKING TIME: 1 hour
SERVES 4

300 ml stock (fish, chicken or vegetable)
1 stem lemon grass, bruised
4 fresh kaffir lime leaves, finely shredded
2 tablespoons vegetable oil
1 small red onion, thinly sliced
1½–2 tablespoons good-quality Thai red curry paste
1½ cups (330 g) arborio rice
300 ml coconut cream
600 g raw prawns, peeled and deveined with tails intact

1 Preheat the oven to moderate 180°C (350°F/Gas 4). Pour the stock into a saucepan, add the lemon grass and half of the kaffir lime leaves. Bring to the boil, then reduce the heat and simmer, covered, for 10 minutes.

2 Heat the oil in a flameproof casserole dish with a lid. Add the onion and cook over medium–low heat for 4–5 minutes, or until soft but not coloured. Stir in the curry paste and cook for a further minute, or until fragrant. Stir in the rice until well coated. Strain the stock into the rice then add the coconut cream. Cover and bake for 15 minutes.

3 Remove from the oven, stir the risotto well, then bake for a further 10–15 minutes. Add the prawns and mix them well into the rice—if the mixture looks a little dry add ½ cup (125 ml) stock or water. Bake for a further 10–15 minutes, or until the prawns are cooked through and the rice is tender. Serve the risotto in bowls garnished with the remaining shredded lime leaves.

Strain stock mixture into rice mixture, then add coconut cream.

Add prawns and mix well into risotto, adding stock if necessary.

Gnocchi with Creamy Gorgonzola and Sage Sauce

PREPARATION TIME: 15 minutes
COOKING TIME: 20 minutes
SERVES 4

2 x 500 g packets purchased potato gnocchi
60 g butter
2 cloves garlic, crushed
½ cup (10 g) fresh small sage leaves
100 g gorgonzola cheese
150 ml cream
1 cup (100 g) grated Parmesan

1 Preheat the grill to high. Lightly grease four 1 cup (250 ml) heatproof gratin dishes. Cook the gnocchi in a large saucepan of rapidly boiling salted water according to the packet instructions until al dente. Lift the gnocchi out with a slotted spoon, leave to drain, then divide among the prepared dishes.

2 Melt the butter in a small saucepan over medium heat, add the garlic and sage leaves and cook for a few minutes, or until the leaves start to crispen and the garlic browns a little. Pour the sage butter evenly over the gnocchi in the gratin dishes.

3 Dot small knobs of the gorgonzola evenly among the gnocchi. Pour the cream over the top of each dish and sprinkle with the Parmesan. Place the dishes under the grill and cook until the top starts to brown and the gnocchi are heated through. Serve with a fresh green salad.

Cook butter, garlic and sage until sage crispens and garlic browns.

Dot knobs of gorgonzola evenly over gnocchi.

Spanish Saffron Chicken and Rice

PREPARATION TIME: 10 minutes
COOKING TIME: 1 hour
SERVES 4

¼ cup (60 ml) olive oil
4 chicken thighs and 6 drumsticks
1 large red onion, finely chopped
1 large green capsicum, two thirds diced
  and one third julienned
3 teaspoons sweet paprika
400 g can diced tomatoes
1¼ cups (275 g) paella or arborio rice
½ teaspoon ground saffron

1 Heat 2 tablespoons of the oil in a large deep frying pan over high heat. Season the chicken pieces well and brown in batches. Remove the chicken from the pan.

2 Reduce the pan to medium heat and add the remaining oil. Add the onion and the diced capsicum and cook gently for 5 minutes. Stir in the paprika and cook for 30 seconds. Add the tomato and simmer for 1–3 minutes, or until it thickens.

3 Stir in 3½ cups (875 ml) boiling water to the pan, then add the rice and saffron. Return the chicken to the pan and stir to combine. Season to taste. Bring to the boil, then cover, reduce the heat to medium–low and simmer for 20–30 minutes, or until all the liquid has been absorbed and the chicken is tender. Stir in the julienned capsicum, then allow to stand, covered, for 3–4 minutes before serving.

Simmer onion, capsicum, paprika and tomato until mixture thickens.

Add water and saffron, return chicken to pan and stir to combine.

Rosemary and Red Wine Steaks with Barbecued Vegetables

PREPARATION TIME: 15 minutes +
25 minutes marinating
COOKING TIME: 45 minutes
SERVES 4

12 small new potatoes
¼ cup (60 ml) olive oil
1 tablespoon finely chopped fresh rosemary
6 cloves garlic, sliced
sea salt flakes, to season
4 large, thick field mushrooms
12 asparagus spears
1 cup (250 ml) red wine
4 scotch fillet steaks (about 260 g each)

1 Heat a barbecue plate or chargrill pan to hot. Toss the potatoes with 1 tablespoon of the oil, half the rosemary and half the garlic and season with the sea salt flakes. Divide the potatoes among four large sheets of foil (three potatoes per sheet) and wrap up into neat packages, sealing firmly around the edges. Place on the barbecue and cook, turning frequently for about 30–40 minutes, or until tender.

2 Meanwhile, brush the mushrooms and asparagus with a little of the remaining oil and set aside.

3 Combine the red wine with the remaining oil, rosemary and garlic in a non-metallic dish. Season with lots of freshly ground black pepper. Add the steaks and turn to coat well in the marinade. Allow to marinate for 25 minutes, then drain.

4 Place the steaks on the barbecue with the mushrooms and cook for 4 minutes each side, or until cooked to your liking (this will depend on the thickness of your steak). Transfer the steaks and mushrooms to a plate, cover lightly and allow o rest. Add the asparagus to the barbecue, .urning regularly for about 2 minutes, or until tender. By this stage your potatoes should be cooked—open the foil and pierce with a skewer to check for doneness. Season with salt and pepper. Serve a steak per person, accompanied by a mushroom, three asparagus spears and a potato package.

Divide potatoes among 4 sheets of foil, wrap and seal firmly.

Barbecue steaks and mushrooms, then transfer to a plate to rest.

Barbecued Chermoula Prawns

PREPARATION TIME: 15 minutes +
10 minutes standing
COOKING TIME: 10 minutes
SERVES 4

1 kg raw medium prawns
3 teaspoons hot paprika
2 teaspoons ground cumin
1 cup (30 g) firmly packed fresh flat-leaf
   parsley
½ cup (15 g) firmly packed fresh coriander
   leaves
100 ml lemon juice
145 ml olive oil
1½ cups (280 g) couscous
1 tablespoon grated lemon rind
lemon wedges, to serve

1 Peel the prawns, leaving the tails intact. Gently
pull out the dark vein from the backs, starting at
the head end. Place the prawns in a large bowl.
Dry-fry the paprika and cumin in a frying pan for
about 1 minute, or until fragrant. Remove from
the heat.

2 Blend or process the spices, parsley, coriander,
lemon juice and ½ cup (125 ml) of the oil until
finely chopped. Add a little salt and pepper. Pour
over the prawns and mix well, then cover with
plastic wrap and refrigerate for 10 minutes. Heat
a chargrill pan or barbecue plate to hot.

3 Meanwhile, to cook the couscous, bring 1 cup
(250 ml) water to the boil in a saucepan, then stir
in the couscous, lemon rind, the remaining oil and
¼ teaspoon salt. Remove from the heat, cover and
leave for 5 minutes. Fluff the couscous with
a fork, adding a little extra olive oil if needed.

4 Cook the prawns on the chargrill pan for about
3–4 minutes, or until cooked through, turning and
brushing with extra marinade while cooking (take
care not to overcook). Serve the prawns on a bed
of couscous, with a wedge of lemon.

*Fry paprika and cumin for about
1 minute, until fragrant.*

Tandoori Chicken with Cardamom Rice

PREPARATION TIME: 15 minutes + 30 minutes
soaking + 10 minutes marinating
COOKING TIME: 25 minutes
SERVES 4

200 g plain yoghurt, plus extra for serving
¼ cup (60 g) good-quality tandoori paste
2 tablespoons lemon juice
1 kg chicken breast fillets, cut into 3 cm
    cubes
1 tablespoon oil
1 onion, finely diced
1½ cups (300 g) long-grain rice
2 cardamom pods, bruised
3 cups (750 ml) hot chicken stock
400 g English spinach leaves

1 Soak eight wooden skewers in water for 30 minutes to prevent them burning during cooking. Combine the yoghurt, tandoori paste and lemon juice in a non-metallic dish. Add the chicken and coat well, then cover and marinate for at least 10 minutes.

2 Meanwhile, heat the oil in a saucepan. Add the onion and cook for 3 minutes, then add the rice and cardamom pods. Cook, stirring often, for 3–5 minutes, or until the rice is slightly opaque. Add the stock and bring to the boil. Reduce the heat to low, cover, and cook, without removing the lid, for 15 minutes.

3 Heat a barbecue plate or oven grill to very hot. Thread the chicken cubes onto the skewers, leaving the bottom quarter of the skewers empty. Cook on each side for 4–5 minutes, or until cooked through.

4 Wash the spinach and place in a large saucepan with just the water clinging to the leaves. Cook, covered, over medium heat for 1–2 minutes, or until the spinach has wilted. Uncover the rice, fluff with a fork and serve with the spinach, chicken and extra yoghurt.

Thread marinated chicken onto skewers.

Barbecued Asian Pork Ribs with Spring Onion Rice

PREPARATION TIME: 15 minutes +
10 minutes marinating
COOKING TIME: 40 minutes
SERVES 4

1 kg American-style pork ribs, cut into
  sections of 4–5 ribs
¼ cup (60 ml) hoisin sauce
1 tablespoon Chinese rice wine or dry sherry
¼ cup (60 ml) soy sauce
2 cloves garlic, chopped
2 tablespoons oil
3 spring onions, finely chopped
1 tablespoon grated fresh ginger
1¼ cups (250 g) jasmine rice
600 g baby bok choy, leaves separated

1 Place the ribs in a non-metallic bowl. Combine the hoisin sauce, rice wine, soy sauce, garlic, 1 table-spoon of the oil, 2 tablespoons of the spring onion and half the ginger. Pour onto the ribs and mix to coat. Marinate for at least 10 minutes, or overnight in the refrigerator.

2 Bring a large saucepan of water to the boil. Add the rice and cook for 12 minutes, stirring occasionally. Drain well.

3 Heat the remaining oil in a small saucepan over medium–low heat. When the oil is warm but not smoking, remove the pan from the heat and add the remaining spring onion and ginger. Season with ¼ teaspoon salt, stirring quickly to combine. Stir this mixture through the rice.

4 Preheat a chargrill pan or barbecue plate and brush with oil. Remove the ribs from the marinade with tongs and reserve the marinade. Cook the ribs in batches, if necessary, for 8–10 minutes on each side, or until cooked through, basting with the marinade during cooking.

5 Five minutes before the ribs are cooked, place the reserved marinade in a saucepan and bring to the boil (add ⅓ cup/80 ml water if there is not much liquid). Boil for 2 minutes, then add the bok choy, stirring to coat. Cook, covered, for 1–2 minutes, or until just wilted. Serve the ribs with the rice and bok choy, and drizzle with the marinade.

Heat oil in a pan until warm, then add spring onion and ginger.

Cook ribs in batches, basting with marinade while cooking.

Cajun Chicken with Fresh Tomato and Corn Salsa

PREPARATION TIME: 15 minutes
COOKING TIME: 15 minutes
SERVES 4

2 corn cobs
2 vine-ripened tomatoes, diced
1 Lebanese cucumber, diced
2 tablespoons roughly chopped fresh
    coriander leaves
4 chicken breast fillets (about 200 g each)
¼ cup (35 g) Cajun seasoning
2 tablespoons lime juice
lime wedges, to serve

1 Cook the corn cobs in a saucepan of boiling water for 5 minutes, or until tender. Remove the kernels using a sharp knife and place in a bowl with the tomato, cucumber and coriander. Season and mix well.

2 Heat a chargrill pan or barbecue plate to medium heat and brush lightly with oil. Pound each chicken breast between two sheets of plastic wrap with a mallet or rolling pin until 2 cm thick. Lightly coat the chicken with the Cajun seasoning and shake off any excess. Cook for 5 minutes on each side, or until just cooked through.

3 Just before serving, stir the lime juice into the salsa. Place a chicken breast on each serving plate and spoon the salsa on the side. Serve with the lime wedges, a green salad and crusty bread.

Remove corn kernels from cooked cobs using a sharp knife.

Lightly coat chicken with Cajun seasoning and shake off excess.

Vegetable Skewers with Basil Couscous

PREPARATION TIME: 15 minutes + 30 minutes
soaking + 10 minutes standing
COOKING TIME: 15 minutes
SERVES 4

5 thin zucchini, cut into 2 cm cubes
5 slender eggplants, cut into 2 cm cubes
12 button mushrooms, halved
2 red capsicums, cut into 1.5 cm cubes
250 g kefalotyri cheese, cut into 2 cm thick
   pieces
⅓ cup (80 ml) lemon juice
2 garlic cloves, finely chopped
5 tablespoons finely chopped fresh basil
145 ml extra virgin olive oil
1 cup (185 g) couscous
1 teaspoon grated lemon rind

1 Soak 12 wooden skewers in water for 30 minutes to prevent them burning during cooking. Thread alternate pieces of vegetables and kefalotyri, starting and finishing with a piece of capsicum and using two pieces of kefalotyri per skewer. Place in a non-metallic dish large enough to hold them in one layer.

2 Combine the lemon juice, garlic, 4 tablespoons of the basil and ½ cup (125 ml) of the oil in a non-metallic bowl. Season. Pour two thirds of the marinade over the skewers, reserving the remainder. Turn the skewers to coat evenly, cover with plastic wrap and marinate for at least 5 minutes.

3 Place the couscous, lemon rind and 1½ cups (375 ml) boiling water in a large heatproof bowl. Stand for 5 minutes, or until all the water has been absorbed. Add the remaining oil and basil, then fluff gently with a fork to separate the grains. Cover.

4 Meanwhile, heat a chargrill pan or barbecue plate to medium–high. Cook the skewers, brushing often with the leftover marinade in the non-metallic dish, for 4–5 minutes on each side, or until the vegetables are cooked and the cheese browns—take care that the cheese doesn't fall apart during cooking.

5 Divide the couscous and skewers among four serving plates. Season, then drizzle with the reserved marinade to taste. Serve immediately with lemon wedges, if desired.

Lamb Cutlets with Mint Gremolata

PREPARATION TIME: 15 minutes
COOKING TIME: 10 minutes
SERVES 4

4 tablespoons fresh mint leaves
1 tablespoon fresh flat-leaf parsley
2 cloves garlic
1½ tablespoons lemon rind (white pith removed), cut into thin strips
2 tablespoons extra virgin olive oil
8 French-trimmed lamb cutlets
2 carrots
2 zucchini
1 tablespoon lemon juice

1 To make the gremolata, finely chop the mint, parsley, garlic and lemon strips, then combine well.

2 Heat a chargrill pan or barbecue plate to very hot. Lightly brush with 1 tablespoon of the oil. Cook the cutlets over medium heat for 2 minutes on each side, or until cooked to your liking. Remove the cutlets and cover to keep warm.

3 Trim the ends from the carrots and zucchini and, using a sharp vegetable peeler, peel the vegetables lengthways into ribbons. Heat the remaining oil in a large saucepan, add the vegetables and toss over medium heat for 3–5 minutes, or until sautéed but tender.

4 Divide the cutlets among the serving plates, sprinkle the cutlets with the gremolata and drizzle with the lemon juice. Serve with the vegetable ribbons.

Finely chop mint, parsley, garlic and lemon strips, then combine.

Peel carrots and zucchini into ribbons using a vegetable peeler.

Swordfish with Tomato Salsa and Garlic Mash

PREPARATION TIME: 15 minutes

COOKING TIME: 25 minutes

SERVES 4

500 g potatoes, cubed
2 large vine-ripened tomatoes
2 tablespoons finely shredded fresh basil
1 tablespoon balsamic vinegar
3 cloves garlic, finely chopped
145 ml olive oil
4 swordfish steaks (about 200 g each)

1 Cook the potato in a large saucepan of boiling water for 12–15 minutes, or until tender.

2 To make the salsa, score a cross in the base of each tomato. Place in a heatproof bowl and cover with boiling water. Leave for 30 seconds, then plunge into iced water and peel the skin away from the cross. Cut the tomatoes in half, scoop out the seeds with a teaspoon and discard. Finely dice the flesh, then combine with the basil, vinegar, 2 cloves of the garlic and 2 tablespoons of the oil. Season.

3 Heat ¼ cup (60 ml) of the olive oil in a large non-stick frying pan over medium–high heat. Season the swordfish well, then add to the frying pan and cook for 2–3 minutes on each side for medium–rare, or until cooked to your liking.

4 Just before the swordfish is ready, drain the potato. Add the remaining olive oil and garlic, and season to taste. Mash until smooth with a potato masher.

5 To serve, put the swordfish steaks on four serving plates and top with the tomato salsa. Serve the garlic mash on the side.

Cut a cross in the base of tomato, then cover with boiling water.

Stuffed Chicken Breast with Goat's Cheese and Asparagus

PREPARATION TIME: 15 minutes
COOKING TIME: 20 minutes
SERVES 4

4 large chicken breast fillets
100 g semi-dried tomatoes
100 g mild goat's cheese, sliced
200 g asparagus spears, trimmed, halved
  and blanched
50 g butter
1½ cups (375 ml) chicken stock
2 zucchini, cut into 5 cm batons
1 cup (250 ml) cream
8 spring onions, thinly sliced

1 Pound each chicken breast between two sheets of plastic wrap with a mallet or rolling pin until 1 cm thick. Divide the tomato, goat's cheese and 155 g of the asparagus pieces among the breasts. Roll up tightly lengthways, securing along the seam with toothpicks.

2 Heat the butter in a large frying pan over medium heat. Add the chicken, then brown on all sides. Pour in the stock, then reduce the heat to low. Cook, covered, for 10 minutes, or until the chicken is cooked through. Remove the chicken and keep warm.

3 Meanwhile, bring a saucepan of lightly salted water to the boil. Add the zucchini and remaining asparagus and cook for 2 minutes, or until just tender. Remove from the pan.

4 Whisk the cream into the frying pan. Add the spring onion and simmer over medium–low heat for 4 minutes, or until reduced and thickened.

5 To serve, cut each chicken roll in half on the diagonal and place on serving plates. Spoon on the sauce and serve with the greens.

Place tomato, goat's cheese and asparagus on flattened chicken.

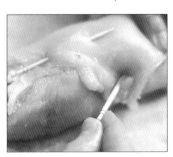

Roll up tightly lengthways and secure with toothpicks.

Tofu, Snow Pea and Mushroom Stir-fry

PREPARATION TIME: 10 minutes
COOKING TIME: 15 minutes
SERVES 4

1¼ cups (250 g) jasmine rice
¼ cup (60 ml) peanut oil
600 g firm tofu, drained, cut into 2 cm cubes
2 teaspoons sambal oelek or chilli paste
2 cloves garlic, finely chopped
400 g fresh Asian mushrooms, sliced (shiitake, oyster or black fungus)
300 g snow peas, trimmed
¼ cup (60 ml) kecap manis

1 Bring a large saucepan of water to the boil. Add the rice and cook for 12 minutes, stirring occasionally. Drain well.

2 Meanwhile, heat a wok until very hot. Add 2 tablespoons of the oil and swirl to coat. Stir-fry the tofu in two batches on all sides for 2–3 minutes, or until lightly browned, then transfer to a plate.

3 Add the remaining oil to the wok, add the sambal oelek, garlic, mushrooms, snow peas and 1 table-spoon water and stir-fry for 1–2 minutes, or until the vegetables are almost cooked but still crunchy.

4 Return the tofu to the wok, add the kecap manis and stir-fry for another minute, or until heated through and combined. Serve immediately with the rice.

Stir-fry tofu in a hot wok until lightly browned.

Stir-fry vegetables until cooked but still crunchy.

Teriyaki Chicken with Ginger Chive Rice

PREPARATION TIME: 10 minutes +
1 hour marinating
COOKING TIME: 20 minutes
SERVES 4

4 small chicken breast fillets, skin on (about
  170 g each)
¼ cup (60 ml) Japanese soy sauce
2 tablespoons sake
1½ tablespoons mirin
1½ tablespoons soft brown sugar
3 teaspoons finely grated fresh ginger
1½ cups (300 g) long-grain rice
2 tablespoons finely chopped fresh chives
2 tablespoons oil

1 Pound each breast between two sheets of plastic wrap with a mallet or rolling pin until 1 cm thick.

2 Place the soy sauce, sake, mirin, sugar and 1 teaspoon of the ginger in a flat non-metallic dish big enough to fit all the chicken in a single layer and stir until the sugar has dissolved. Add the chicken and turn to coat. Cover and refrigerate for 1 hour, turning once halfway through.

3 Once the chicken has marinated, bring a large saucepan of water to the boil. Add the rice and cook for 12 minutes, stirring occasionally. Drain. Stir in the chives and the remaining ginger, then cover until ready to serve.

4 Meanwhile, drain the chicken, reserving the marinade. Heat the oil in a large deep frying pan and cook the chicken, skin-side-down over medium heat for 4–5 minutes, or until the skin is crisp. Turn and cook the other side for 4 minutes—remove from the pan (the chicken should not be quite cooked through).

5 Add the reserved marinade and ¼ cup (60 ml) water to the pan and scrape any sediment stuck to the base. Bring to the boil over high heat, then return the chicken (skin-side-up) with any juices to the pan. Cook for 5–6 minutes, or until just cooked through, turning once to coat. (If the sauce is still a little runny, remove the chicken and boil the sauce over high heat until it is slightly syrupy.) Rest the chicken for a few minutes.

6 To serve, divide the rice among four serving plates and place the chicken (either whole or sliced on the diagonal) on top. Drizzle with a little sauce and serve with steamed Asian greens.

Veal Scaloppine with Sage

PREPARATION TIME: 15 minutes
COOKING TIME: 1 hour
SERVES 4

600 g small new potatoes, halved
⅓ cup (80 ml) olive oil
8 small (600 g) veal scaloppine fillets or schnitzels
4 slices pancetta, cut in half lengthways
8 fresh sage leaves
1 cup (250 ml) Marsala
250 g asparagus spears

1 Preheat the oven to moderately hot 200°C (400°F/Gas 6). Cook the potatoes in a large saucepan of boiling water for 10 minutes. Drain and transfer to a baking tray with 2 tablespoons of the olive oil. Toss well and bake for 40–50 minutes, or until crisp.

2 Meanwhile, pound each veal fillet between two sheets of plastic wrap with a mallet or rolling pin until 5 mm thick. Press a piece of pancetta and a sage leaf onto each scaloppine fillet, then skewer with a toothpick. Season well with salt and freshly ground black pepper.

3 Heat the remaining oil in a large heavy-based frying pan. Place the scaloppine pancetta-side-down in the pan and cook for 1–2 minutes. Turn and cook for another minute. Remove from the pan and keep warm (you may have to do this in two batches). Add the Marsala and cook for 4–5 minutes, or until syrupy and reduced by half. Return the scaloppine to the pan and toss lightly in the sauce until warmed through.

4 When the potatoes are nearly ready, bring a large saucepan of lightly salted water to the boil. Add the asparagus and cook for 3 minutes. Drain.

5 To serve, remove the toothpicks from the scaloppine and divide among four serving plates. Drizzle any pan juices on top. Serve with the asparagus and roast potatoes on the side.

Press a piece of pancetta and a sage leaf to each fillet and secure.

Pan-fried Lamb Fillets with Red Wine

PREPARATION TIME: 10 minutes
COOKING TIME: 20 minutes
SERVES 4

600 g small new potatoes
160 g snow peas, trimmed
2 tablespoons olive oil
4 lamb backstraps or eye of loin fillets
  (about 200 g each), trimmed
⅔ cup (170 ml) red wine
1 tablespoon redcurrant jelly
2 teaspoons chopped fresh thyme
30 g butter, chilled and cut into cubes

1 Cook the potatoes in a large saucepan of lightly salted boiling water for 15–20 minutes, or until tender. Add the snow peas and cook for a further 1 minute. Drain the vegetables, return to the pan and toss gently with 1 tablespoon of the oil.

2 Meanwhile, heat the remaining oil in a large frying pan and cook the lamb fillets over medium–high heat for 4–5 minutes, or until cooked, but still pink inside. Remove from the pan, cover and keep warm.

3 Add the wine, redcurrant jelly and thyme to the pan and bring to the boil. Boil rapidly for 5 minutes, or until reduced and syrupy. Stir in the butter.

4 To serve, slice the lamb on the diagonal, divide among four plates and spoon some of the sauce on top. Serve with the vegetables.

Combine wine, redcurrant jelly and thyme and boil until syrupy.

Salt and Pepper Chicken with Asian Greens and Oyster Sauce

PREPARATION TIME: 15 minutes
COOKING TIME: 20 minutes
SERVES 4

1¼ cups (250 g) jasmine rice
⅓ cup (40 g) plain flour
¾ teaspoon five-spice powder
1½ teaspoons fine sea salt
1 teaspoon ground white pepper
750 g chicken breast fillets, cut into thin
   strips (1 cm x 5 cm)
145 ml peanut oil
1.25 kg mixed Asian greens (bok choy, choy
   sum or gai larn)
½ cup (125 ml) oyster sauce

1 Preheat the oven to moderately hot 200°C (400°F/Gas 6). Bring a large saucepan of water to the boil. Add the rice and cook for 12 minutes, stirring occasionally. Drain well.

2 Meanwhile, combine the flour, five-spice powder, salt and pepper in a large bowl. Toss the chicken strips in the flour until well coated. Heat ¼ cup (60 ml) of the oil in a large frying pan over medium–high heat. Add the chicken in three batches and cook, turning, for about 3 minutes, or until browned. Drain on crumpled paper towels and keep warm.

3 Heat the remaining oil and cook the mixed Asian greens over medium–high heat for 1–2 minutes. Add the oyster sauce and toss through. Serve on a bed of jasmine rice topped with the chicken strips.

Prawns with Spicy Tamarind Sauce

PREPARATION TIME: 15 minutes
COOKING TIME: 25 minutes
SERVES 4

½ cup (80 g) raw cashew nuts
1¼ cups (250 g) jasmine rice
2 garlic cloves, finely chopped
1½ tablespoons fish sauce
1 tablespoon sambal oelek
1 tablespoon peanut oil
1 kg raw medium prawns, peeled and
  deveined with tails intact
2 teaspoons tamarind concentrate
1½ tablespoons grated palm sugar
350 g choy sum, cut into 10 cm lengths

1 Preheat the oven to moderate 180°C (350°F/Gas 4). Spread the cashews on a baking tray and bake for 5–8 minutes, or until lightly golden—watch carefully, as they will burn easily.

2 Meanwhile, bring a large saucepan of water to the boil. Add the rice and cook for 12 minutes, stirring occasionally. Drain well.

3 Place the garlic, fish sauce, sambal oelek and toasted cashews in a blender or food processor, adding 2–3 tablespoons of water, if needed, and blend to a rough paste.

4 Heat a wok until very hot, add the oil and swirl to coat. Add the prawns, toss for 1–2 minutes, or until starting to turn pink. Remove from the wok. Add the cashew paste and stir-fry for 1 minute, or until it starts to brown slightly. Add the tamarind, sugar and about ⅓ cup (80 ml) water, then bring to the boil, stirring well. Return the prawns to the wok and stir to coat. Cook for 2–3 minutes, or until the prawns are cooked through.

5 Place the choy sum in a paper-lined bamboo steamer and steam over a wok or saucepan of simmering water for 3 minutes, or until tender. Serve with the prawns and rice.

Stir-fry cashew paste for 1 minute, then add tamarind and sugar.

Lemon Grass Beef

PREPARATION TIME: 15 minutes +
10 minutes marinating
COOKING TIME: 25 minutes
SERVES 4

1½ cups (300 g) long-grain rice
3 cloves garlic, finely chopped
1 tablespoon grated fresh ginger
4 stems lemon grass (white part only), finely
  chopped
2½ tablespoons oil
600 g lean rump steak, trimmed and sliced
  thinly across the grain
1 tablespoon lime juice
1–2 tablespoons fish sauce
2 tablespoons kecap manis
1 large red onion, cut into small wedges
200 g green beans, sliced on the diagonal
  into 5 cm lengths

1 Bring a large saucepan of water to the boil. Add the rice and cook for 12 minutes, stirring occasionally. Drain well.

2 Meanwhile, combine the garlic, ginger, lemon grass and 2 teaspoons of the oil in a non-metallic bowl. Add the beef, then marinate for 10 minutes. Combine the lime juice, fish sauce and kecap manis.

3 Heat a wok until very hot, add 1 tablespoon oil and swirl to coat. Stir-fry the beef in batches for 2–3 minutes, or until browned. Remove from the wok.

4 Reheat the wok to very hot, heat the remaining oil, then add the onion and stir-fry for 2 minutes. Add the beans and cook for another 2 minutes, then return the beef to the wok. Pour in the fish sauce mixture and cook until heated through. Serve with the rice.

Pour fish sauce mixture over beef and beans and heat through.

Ginger Chicken Stir-Fry with Hokkien Noodles

PREPARATION TIME: 15 minutes +
5 minutes soaking
COOKING TIME: 10 minutes
SERVES 4

2½ tablespoons finely shredded fresh
  ginger
¼ cup (60 ml) mirin
2 tablespoons soy sauce
600 g chicken tenderloins or chicken breast
  fillets, cut diagonally into thin strips
180 g fresh baby corn
350 g choy sum
150 g fresh oyster mushrooms
500 g Hokkien noodles, gently separated
2 tablespoons oil
2 tablespoons oyster sauce

1 Combine the ginger, mirin and soy sauce in a non-metallic bowl. Add the chicken, coat well, then marinate while preparing the vegetables.

2 Cut the corn in half lengthways; trim the ends off the choy sum and cut into 6 cm lengths. If the mushrooms are very large, cut them in half. Soak the noodles in a large heatproof bowl in boiling water for 5 minutes. Drain and refresh under cold running water.

3 Heat a wok until very hot, add 1 tablespoon of the oil and swirl to coat. Remove the chicken from the marinade with a slotted spoon and cook in two batches over very high heat for 2 minutes, or until brown and just cooked. Remove from the wok.

4 Add the remaining oil to the wok and stir-fry the mushrooms and corn for 1–2 minutes, or until just softened. Add the remaining marinade, bring to the boil, then add the chicken, choy sum and noodles. Stir in the oyster sauce and cook, tossing well, for 1–2 minutes, or until the choy sum has wilted slightly and the noodles are warmed through.

Soak noodles in boiling water, then refresh under cold running water.

Remove chicken from marinade using a slotted spoon.

Paprika Veal with Caraway Noodles

PREPARATION TIME: 10 minutes
COOKING TIME: 1 hour 35 minutes
SERVES 4

3 tablespoons oil
1 kg veal shoulder, diced
1 large onion, thinly sliced
3 cloves garlic, finely chopped
¼ cup (60 g) Hungarian paprika
½ teaspoon caraway seeds
2 x 400 g cans chopped tomatoes, one drained
350 g fresh fettuccine
40 g butter, softened

1 Heat half the oil in a large saucepan over medium–high heat, then brown the veal in batches for 3 minutes per batch. Remove the veal from the pan and set aside with any pan juices.

2 Add the remaining oil to the pan and sauté the onion and garlic over medium heat for 5 minutes, or until softened. Add the paprika and ¼ teaspoon of the caraway seeds and stir for 30 seconds.

3 Add the chopped tomatoes and their liquid plus ½ cup (125 ml) water. Return the veal to the pan with any juices, increase the heat to high and bring to the boil. Reduce the heat to low, then cover and simmer for 1 hour 15 minutes, or until the meat is tender and the sauce has thickened.

4 About 15 minutes before the veal is ready, cook the pasta in a large saucepan of rapidly boiling salted water according to the packet instructions until al dente. Drain, then return to the pan. Stir in the butter and the remaining caraway seeds. Serve immediately with the paprika veal.

Brown the veal in batches for 3 minutes per batch; set aside.

Simmer tomatoes and veal until meat is tender and sauce is thick.

Beef and Red Wine Stew

PREPARATION TIME: 10 minutes
COOKING TIME: 2 hours
SERVES 4

1 kg diced beef
¼ cup (30 g) seasoned plain flour
1 tablespoon oil
150 g bacon, diced
8 bulb spring onions, greens
  trimmed to 2 cm
200 g button mushrooms
2 cups (500 ml) red wine
2 tablespoons tomato paste
2 cups (500 ml) beef stock
1 bouquet garni

1 Toss the beef in the seasoned flour until evenly coated, shaking off any excess. Heat the oil in a large saucepan over high heat. Cook the beef in three batches for about 3 minutes, or until well browned all over, adding a little extra oil as needed. Remove from the pan.

2 Add the bacon to the pan and cook for 2 minutes, or until browned. Remove with a slotted spoon and add to the beef. Add the spring onions and mushrooms and cook for 5 minutes, or until the onions are browned. Remove.

3 Slowly pour the red wine into the pan, scraping up any sediment from the bottom with a wooden spoon. Stir in the tomato paste and stock. Add the bouquet garni and return the beef, bacon and any juices. Bring to the boil, then reduce the heat and simmer for 45 minutes, then return the spring onions and mushrooms to the pan. Cook for 1 hour, or until the meat is very tender and the sauce is glossy. Serve with steamed new potatoes or mash.

Toss beef in seasoned flour until evenly coated; shake off excess.

Slowly pour wine into pan, combining with any pan sediment.

Chicken and Cider Stew with Apple and Potato Mash

PREPARATION TIME: 15 minutes
COOKING TIME: 55 minutes
SERVES 4

1 kg chicken thigh fillets, trimmed and cut into 2 cm cubes
1½ tablespoons finely chopped fresh thyme
1 tablespoon oil
90 g butter
3 French shallots, thinly sliced
1½ cups (375 ml) apple cider
1 kg potatoes, cubed
2 large green apples, peeled, cored and sliced into eighths
⅔ cup (170 ml) cream

1 Season the chicken thighs with 2 teaspoons of the thyme and salt and black pepper. Heat the oil and 20 g of the butter in a large saucepan over medium–high heat. Cook the chicken in two batches for 2–3 minutes, or until evenly browned. Remove from the pan.

2 Add the French shallots and the remaining thyme to the pan and sauté for 2 minutes. Pour in the cider, then bring to the boil, scraping off any sediment that has stuck to the bottom of the pan. Return the chicken to the pan and cover. Reduce the heat to medium–low and cook for 35–40 minutes, or until the chicken is tender and the sauce has reduced (check occasionally to see if any water needs to be added).

3 Meanwhile, cook the potato and apple in a saucepan of boiling water for 15–20 minutes, or until tender. Drain and return to the pan over low heat for a minute to allow any water to evaporate. Remove from the heat, and mash with a potato masher. Stir in 2 tablespoons of the cream and the remaining butter with a wooden spoon, then season well with salt and pepper.

4 Gently stir the remaining cream into the chicken stew and cook for a further 2–4 minutes, or until the sauce has thickened. Serve at once with the potato and apple mash and a crisp green salad.

Pour cider into pan, scraping pan to combine any sediment.

Cook until chicken is tender and the sauce has reduced.

Vegetable Tagine with Couscous

PREPARATION TIME: 15 minutes +
5 minutes standing
COOKING TIME: 40 minutes
SERVES 4

¼ cup (60 ml) olive oil
1 large red capsicum, seeded and
    cut into quarters
1 large eggplant, sliced into 1 cm rounds,
    then in half again
400 g can chopped tomatoes
1 tablespoon harissa paste
1 tablespoon Moroccan spice blend
1 cup (250 ml) vegetable stock
2 large zucchini, cut into 2 cm chunks
1½ cups (225 g) couscous
20 g butter

1 Heat 1 tablespoon of the oil in a saucepan over medium–high heat. Sauté the capsicum, skin-side-down, covered, for 3–4 minutes, or until the skin is well browned. Remove from the pan. Peel off the skin and cut the flesh into 1 cm slices. Heat the remaining oil in the pan and cook the eggplant in batches over medium–high heat for 4–5 minutes, or until well browned. Remove.

2 Return the capsicum to the pan, then stir in the tomato, harissa paste and Moroccan spice blend. Pour in the stock and bring to the boil. Reduce the heat to medium–low and simmer, uncovered, for 15 minutes. Add the zucchini and eggplant and cook for a further 8 minutes, or until the vegetables are tender.

3 About 10 minutes before the vegetables are ready, place the couscous in a heatproof bowl, add 1½ cups (375 ml) boiling water, and leave for 3–5 minutes. Stir in the butter and fluff with a fork until the butter has melted and the grains separate. Serve the vegetable tagine with the couscous.

Stir butter into cooked couscous and fluff with a fork.

Sichuan Chicken

PREPARATION TIME: 10 minutes
COOKING TIME: 25 minutes
SERVES 4

¼ teaspoon five-spice powder
750 g chicken thigh fillets, halved
2 tablespoons peanut oil
1 tablespoon julienned fresh ginger
1 teaspoon Sichuan peppercorns, crushed
1 teaspoon chilli bean paste (toban jiang)
2 tablespoons light soy sauce
1 tablespoon Chinese rice wine
1¼ cups (250 g) jasmine rice
600 g baby bok choy, leaves separated

1 Sprinkle the five-spice powder over the chicken. Heat a wok until very hot, add half the oil and swirl to coat. Add the chicken and cook for 2 minutes each side, or until browned. Remove from the wok.

2 Reduce the heat to medium and cook the ginger for 30 seconds. Add the peppercorns and chilli bean paste. Return the chicken to the wok, add the soy sauce, wine and ½ cup (125 ml) water, then simmer for 15–20 minutes, or until cooked.

3 Meanwhile, bring a large saucepan of water to the boil. Add the rice and cook for 12 minutes, stirring occasionally. Drain well.

4 Heat the remaining oil in a saucepan. Add the bok choy and toss gently for 1 minute, or until the leaves wilt and the stems are tender. Serve with the chicken and rice.

Chilli Con Carne

PREPARATION TIME: 15 minutes
COOKING TIME: 45 minutes
SERVES 4

1 tablespoon oil
1 large red onion, finely chopped
2 cloves garlic, crushed
1½ teaspoons chilli powder
1 teaspoon ground oregano
2 teaspoons ground cumin
500 g lean beef mince
2 x 400 g cans chopped tomatoes
420 g can red kidney beans, drained and
  rinsed
8 flour tortillas
sour cream, to serve, optional

1 Preheat the oven to moderate 180°C (350°F/Gas 4). Heat the oil in a large saucepan, add the onion and garlic and cook, stirring, over medium heat for about 5 minutes, or until softened. Add the chilli powder, oregano and cumin and stir until fragrant. Add the mince and cook, stirring, for about 5 minutes, or until browned all over, breaking up any lumps with the back of a wooden spoon.

2 Add the tomato, beans and ½ cup (125 ml) water and simmer, stirring occasionally, for about 30 minutes, or until thick. Season to taste with salt and pepper. About 10 minutes before serving, wrap the tortillas in foil and heat them in the oven according to packet instructions to soften. Fill the tortillas with the chilli and wrap. Serve with sour cream and, if desired, a green salad.

Fry onion, garlic, chilli power, oregano and cumin until fragrant.

Add mince and cook until browned all over and crumbly.

Lamb Kofta Curry

PREPARATION TIME: 15 minutes
COOKING TIME: 30 minutes
SERVES 4

1¼ cups (250 g) jasmine rice
1 kg lean lamb mince
1 egg, lightly beaten
2 onions, finely chopped
120 g good-quality mild Korma curry paste
4 tablespoons chopped fresh coriander
  leaves
2 cloves garlic, crushed
2 tablespoons oil
400 g can diced tomatoes

1 Preheat the oven to hot 220°C (425°F/Gas 7) and lightly grease two baking trays. Bring a large saucepan of water to the boil. Add the rice and cook for 12 minutes, stirring occasionally. Drain well.

2 Meanwhile, combine the mince, egg, 1 of the onions, 2 tablespoons of the curry paste, 3 tablespoons of the coriander, 1 clove of garlic and salt. Form tablespoons of the mixture into balls and place on one of the prepared baking trays.

3 Heat 1 tablespoon of the oil in a large non-stick frying pan over medium heat. When hot, cook the balls in batches for 1 minute on each side, or until evenly golden, but not cooked through. Place on the second tray and bake for 5–7 minutes, or until cooked through.

4 Meanwhile, wipe the pan clean with paper towels. Heat the remaining oil over medium heat. Add the remaining onion and garlic and cook for 3 minutes, or until the onion is soft. Add the remaining curry paste and cook for 1 minute before adding the tomatoes and 1 cup (250 ml) water. Bring to the boil, then reduce the heat to low and gently simmer for 10 minutes, or until the sauce thickens slightly. Season with salt.

5 Add the baked meatballs and their juices to the sauce, and gently stir, coating in the sauce. Simmer for 5 minutes, or until the meatballs are warmed through. Serve with rice and sprinkle with the remaining coriander.

Form tablespoons of mince mixture into small balls.

Add baked meatball to pan, and stir to coat evenly with sauce.

Chicken, Artichoke and Broad Bean Stew

PREPARATION TIME: 15 minutes
COOKING TIME: 1 hour 25 minutes
SERVES 4

1 cup (155 g) frozen broad beans
8 chicken thighs on the bone (skin removed, optional)
½ cup (60 g) seasoned plain flour
2 tablespoons oil
1 large red onion, cut into small wedges
½ cup (125 ml) dry white wine
1¼ cups (310 ml) chicken stock
2 teaspoons finely chopped fresh rosemary
340 g marinated artichokes, well drained and quartered
800 g potatoes, cut into large chunks
60 g butter

1 Remove the skins from the broad beans. Coat the chicken in the flour, shaking off the excess. Heat the oil in a saucepan or flameproof casserole dish, then brown the chicken in two batches on all sides over medium heat. Remove and drain on crumpled paper towels.

2 Add the onion to the pan and cook for 3–4 minutes, or until soft but not brown. Increase the heat to high, pour in the wine and boil for 2 minutes, or until reduced to a syrup. Stir in 1 cup (250 ml) of the stock and bring just to the boil, then return the chicken to the pan with the rosemary. Reduce the heat to low and simmer, covered, for 45 minutes.

3 Add the artichokes to the pan, increase the heat to high and return to the boil. Reduce to a simmer and cook, uncovered, for 10–15 minutes. Add the beans and cook for a further 5 minutes.

4 Meanwhile, cook the potato in a saucepan of boiling water for 15–20 minutes, or until tender. Drain, then return to the pan. Add the butter and the remaining stock and mash with a potato masher. Serve on the side of the stew.

Remove the skins from the broad beans and set beans aside.

Cook onion in a pan until soft but not brown.

Add chicken to onion, wine and stock and simmer for 45 minutes.

Beef Masala with Coconut Rice

PREPARATION TIME: 15 minutes +
10 minutes standing
COOKING TIME: 1 hour 50 minutes
SERVES 4

1 tablespoon oil
1 kg chuck beef, trimmed and
   cut into 2 cm cubes
1 large onion, thinly sliced
3 cloves garlic, chopped
⅓ cup (80 g) tikka masala
   curry paste
2 teaspoons tamarind concentrate
2 x 400 ml cans coconut milk
4 fresh curry leaves
1½ cups (300 g) jasmine rice

1 To make the beef masala, heat the oil in a large saucepan over high heat. Add the meat and cook in three batches, for 4 minutes per batch, or until evenly browned. Remove from the pan.

2 Reduce the heat to medium, add the onion and cook for 5 minutes. Add the garlic and cook for 1 minute. Stir in the curry paste and tamarind and cook for 30–60 seconds, or until fragrant. Return the beef to the pan, add 550 ml coconut milk and the curry leaves and bring to the boil. Reduce the heat and simmer gently for 1 hour 30 minutes, or until the meat is tender and the sauce has reduced. Check occasionally to ensure that the sauce doesn't stick to the bottom of the pan— add some water if necessary.

3 Meanwhile, to make the coconut rice, wash and thoroughly drain the rice. Place the rice, the remaining coconut milk and 1 cup (250 ml) water in a saucepan. Bring slowly to the boil, stirring constantly, and boil for 1 minute. Reduce the heat to low and cook, covered tightly, for 20 minutes. Remove from the heat and leave, covered, for 10 minutes. Fluff the rice with a fork before serving. To serve, season the curry to taste, remove the curry leaves, if desired, and serve with the rice.

*Simmer beef and curry sauce
mixture until meat is tender.*

Desserts

DURING THE WEEK, DESSERT IS
USUALLY ABANDONED BECAUSE
OF THE EXTRA TIME IT TAKES TO
PREPARE, BUT THESE HOT AND
COLD SWEETS TAKE LITTLE TIME
AT ALL.

CHOCOLATE CHERRY PARFAIT

chocolate ice cream (1–2 scoops each)
400 g can pitted black cherries, drained
lamington or choc-chip flavoured ice
    cream (1–2 scoops each)
⅓ cup (80 ml) good-quality chocolate
    sauce
dark chocolate cherry bar, chopped,
    to garnish

Divide the chocolate ice cream, cherries
and lamington ice cream among four
parfait glasses. Drizzle with the chocolate
sauce and garnish with the chocolate
cherry bar. Serve at once. Serves 4.

BANANA CARAMEL ICE CREAM STACK

400 g pound cake, cut into 1.5 cm thick
    slices (you will need eight slices)
4 rectangular slabs vanilla ice cream
2 large bananas, cut on the diagonal into
    1 cm slices
3 tablespoons good-quality caramel
    sauce, plus extra to drizzle
⅓ cup (50 g) honey-roasted macadamia
    nuts, chopped, plus extra, to garnish

Place a slice of cake on each of four
serving plates, then top each slice with
an ice cream slab. Divide the banana
slices, caramel sauce and chopped nuts
among each serving, then top with
another slice of cake. Drizzle with extra
caramel sauce and scatter with the extra
nuts. Serve immediately. Serves 4.

Note: Any unused cake can be frozen.

INDIVIDUAL MANGO PASSIONFRUIT TRIFLES

60 g plain sponge cake, cut into
    1 cm pieces
2 tablespoons Cointreau
2 small or 1 large mango, cut into bite-
    sized slices
2 tablespoons passionfruit pulp
½ cup (125 ml) ready-made vanilla
    custard l 200 g mascarpone
1 tablespoon icing sugar
passionfruit pulp, extra, to garnish
    (optional)

Divide the cake pieces among four tall
glasses (about 1¼ cups/310 ml). Drizzle
2 teaspoons Cointreau over the cake in
each glass, then leave for 5 minutes.
Arrange half the mango on the cake.
Divide the passionfruit pulp and custard
evenly among the glasses, then top with
the remaining mango slices. Gently
combine the mascarpone and icing sugar
until light and creamy. Just before
serving, dollop the mascarpone mixture
on top and garnish with extra passionfruit. Serve at once. Serves 4.

Note: Another 1–2 tablespoons of
custard can replace the layer of
mascarpone, if preferred.

LIME DELICIOUS PUDDING

¼ cup (60 g) butter, softened
⅓ cup (90 g) caster sugar
3 eggs, separated
1½ teaspoons finely grated lime rind
¼ cup (30 g) self-raising flour
¾ cup (185 ml) milk
¼ cup (60 ml) lime juice
icing sugar, to dust

Preheat the oven to moderate 180°C (350°F/Gas 4) and lightly grease four 1 cup (250 ml) ramekins. Beat the butter, sugar, egg yolks and lime rind with electric beaters until light and creamy. Fold the flour into the mixture in two batches, alternating with the milk and lime juice. Beat the egg whites in a clean, dry bowl, until just stiff, then lightly fold into the pudding mixture until just combined. Spoon into the prepared ramekins and place into a large, deep baking tray. Pour in enough water to come halfway up the side of the ramekins and bake for 25 minutes, or until risen and golden on top. Dust lightly with icing sugar and serve at once. Serves 4.

CHOCOLATE CROISSANT PUDDING

3 eggs
¼ cup (60 g) caster sugar
1¼ cups (310 ml) milk
3 plain croissants, torn into small pieces
100 g rum and raisin dark chocolate, roughly chopped
1 tablespoon mixed peel
1 tablespoon demerara sugar

Preheat the oven to moderate 180°C (350°F/Gas 4). Grease a 1.25 litre rectangular ovenproof dish. Whisk the eggs and sugar together until the sugar dissolves, then whisk in the milk until combined and frothy. Place half the croissants in the prepared dish, scatter the chocolate and mixed peel on top, then pour on half the egg mixture. Repeat with the remaining croissant pieces and egg mixture. Sprinkle the surface with the demerara sugar. Place the dish in a large deep baking tray. Pour in enough water to come halfway up the sides of the dish and bake for 40–45 minutes, or until set and golden on top. Serve with ice cream. Serves 4–6.

APPLE CRUMBLE

6 apples, peeled, cored and finely sliced
2 cinnamon sticks
2 cm x 4 cm piece lemon rind
⅓ cup (60 g) soft brown sugar
50 g chopped unsalted butter
½ cup (60 g) plain flour
2 tablespoons flaked almonds

Preheat the oven to moderately hot 200°C (400°F/Gas 6). Lightly grease a 1.25 litre ovenproof dish. Place the apple, cinnamon sticks, lemon rind, 1 tablespoon of the brown sugar, and ½ cup (125 ml) water in a large saucepan. Simmer, partially covered, over medium heat for 8–10 minutes, or until the apple is tender but still holding its shape. Discard the cinnamon and lemon rind. Transfer the apple mixture to the prepared dish. Mix the plain flour, 40 g of the butter and 2 tablespoons of the brown

sugar in a small bowl with your fingertips, rubbing in the butter until it resembles coarse breadcrumbs. Mix in the almonds until well coated. Sprinkle the crumble mixture over the apples, then scatter the remaining butter and soft brown sugar on top. Bake for 15 minutes, or until golden brown. Serve hot or cold, with custard or ice cream. Serves 4.

CHERRY GALETTES

2 sheets ready-rolled puff pastry
200 g cream cheese, softened
1 tablespoon grated lemon rind
670 g jar morello cherries, drained
¼ cup (80 g) sour cherry jam, melted
thick cream, to serve

Preheat the oven to moderately hot 200°C (400°F/Gas 6). Cut two rounds (14 cm diameter) from each sheet of pastry. Prick each round several times with a fork and place on a large baking tray. Bake for 5 minutes, then cool slightly. Mix the cream cheese and lemon rind together, then divide among the pastry rounds, spreading to leave a 2 cm border around the edge of the pastry. Arrange about ⅓ cup (65 g) cherries on each round, and brush the surface with the melted jam. Bake for 20 minutes, or until the pastry is puffed and golden. Serve hot with a dollop of thick cream. Serves 4.

All our recipes are thoroughly tested in a specially developed test kitchen. Standard metric measuring cups and spoons are used in the development of our recipes. All cup and spoon measurements are level. We have used 60 g (2¼ oz/Grade 3) eggs in all recipes. Sizes of cans vary from manufacturer to manufacturer and between countries – use the can size closest to the one suggested in the recipe.

CONVERSION GUIDE

1 cup = 250 ml (9 fl oz)

1 teaspoon = 5 ml

1 Australian tablespoon = 20 ml (4 teaspoons)

1 UK/US tablespoon = 15 ml (3 teaspoons)

Where temperature ranges are indicated, the lower figure applies to gas ovens, the higher to electric ovens. This allows for the fact that the flame in gas ovens generates a drier heat, which effectively cooks food faster than the moister heat of an electric oven, even if the temperature setting is the same.

DRY MEASURES	LIQUID MEASURES	LINEAR MEASURES
30 g = 1 oz	30 ml = 1 fl oz	6 mm = ¼ inch
250 g = 9 oz	125 ml = 4 fl oz	1 cm = ½ inch
500 g = 1 lb 2 oz	250 ml = 9 fl oz	2.5 cm = 1 inch

	°C	°F	GAS MARK
Very slow	120	250	½
Slow	150	300	2
Mod slow	160	325	3
Moderate	180	350	4
Mod hot	190(g)–210(e)	375–425	5
Hot	200(g)–240(e)	400–475	6
Very hot	230(g)–260(e)	450–525	8

CUP CONVERSIONS – DRY INGREDIENTS

1 cup almonds, slivered whole = 125 g (4½ oz)

1 cup cheese, lightly packed processed cheddar = 155 g (5½ oz)

1 cup wheat flour = 125 g (4½ oz)

1 cup wholemeal flour = 140 g (5 oz)

1 cup minced (ground) meat = 250 g (9 oz)

1 cup pasta shapes = 125 g (4½ oz)

1 cup raisins = 170 g (6 oz)

1 cup rice, short grain, raw = 200 g (7 oz)

1 cup sesame seeds = 160 g (6 oz)

1 cup split peas = 250 g (9 oz)

(g) = gas (e) = electric

Note: For fan-forced ovens, check your appliance manual, but as a general rule, set the oven temperature to 20°C lower than the temperature indicated in the recipe.

INTERNATIONAL GLOSSARY

capsicum	sweet bell pepper	cornflour	cornstarch
chick pea	garbanzo bean	eggplant	aubergine
chilli	chile, chili pepper	spring onion	scallion
		zucchini	courgette

First published in 2004 by Murdoch Books Pty Limited.
Erico House, 6th Floor North, 93-99 Upper Richmond Road, Putney, London, SW15 2TG, United Kingdom.

This edition published in 2006 for Index Books Ltd, Garrard Way, Kettering, NN16 8TD, United Kingdom.

ISBN 1 74045 951 2
Printed by Sing Cheong Printing Co. Ltd. PRINTED IN CHINA.